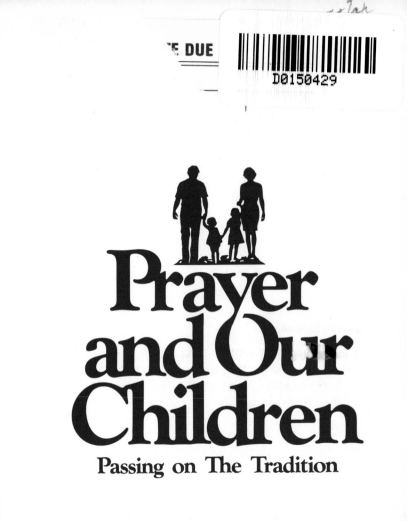

Prayer and Our Children

Passing on The Tradition

MARY TERESE DONZE, ASC

Ave Maria Press • Notre Dame, Indiana 46556

Acknowledgment

Excerpts from THE JERUSALEM BIBLE,
copyright © 1966 by Darton, Longman & Todd,
Ltd. and Doubleday & Company, Inc. Used by
permission of the publisher.

Library of Congress Catalog Card Number: 87-71000

International Standard Book Number: 0-87793-365-0

Printed and bound in the United States of America.

Lovingly dedicated
to
my mother
who first taught me to pray

Contents

About This Book

If you have anything to do with forming the minds and hearts of the children who will be tomorrow's Catholic men and women, this book was written for you.

The content of the book originally formed the material for a talk to a group of Catholic teachers. In order to keep some of the immediateness that is natural in a face-to-face interchange of thought, I have tried to maintain an informal or conversational style. At times I identify with you, the reader, and I find myself saying that it is *we* who need to do certain things; at other times the teacher in me surfaces, and I am telling *you* what to do. I would like to believe this makes for easier reading.

Part One is an appeal to you to preserve for our children those great traditional helps to piety which have nourished our Catholic faith for centuries. It recalls in detail some of these beautiful devotions and practices that form a cherished part of our religious heritage. They are in danger of being lost unless we pass them on to our children, the "twigs" who are given us to bend.

Part Two is a simple guide to making prayer a life style. It is meant to prepare those of us who bend the twig to share more worthily with the Divine Spirit in forming our children to virtue.

God grant that the twigs we bend grow into Cedars of Lebanon.

S.M.T.D.

Part One:
As the Twig Is Bent

As the twig is bent
The tree's inclined
      —Pope

Introduction

The fresh air that came blustering into the church through the windows opened by Vatican II unfortunately blew shut the doors to many popular Catholic devotions and practices with profound effects on the life of faith. This wasn't meant to happen. The council fathers themselves went on record as saying, "Popular devotions of the Christian people are warmly commended . . ." so long as they don't usurp the role of the liturgy.

But, once a window is opened, there's no telling what may happen should a brisk wind rise. When the wind takes on the force of a gale, it's sure to do more than freshen up the house. And now, some 20 years after the church's 21st Ecumenical Council, we find Peter's Barque swept fairly clean of many traditional devotions and practices.

There are those who feel this is as it should be. We have the Mass, they say. We are making more of the Mass than we formerly did, and nothing can replace the Mass. It should be the radiant center of our Catholic devotion.

But the Mass can't bear the burden that's being put on it. The majority of practicing Catholics get to Mass only on Sundays. It is impossible to put into that time all the instruction and inspiration necessary to "Christianize" the rest of the week. We need other devotions to prepare our hearts to be receptive to the graces of the Mass, to keep us in a Christian frame of mind and to support our prayer life.

Some of the devotions and practices suggested here may be more helpful to you than others. What you won't want to do is overemphasize any of them. None is sacrosanct. I make a point of this because in offering suggestions about devotional practices there is always the risk that someone may have a strong attraction to these peripheral means of living one's faith and fail to understand that they are valuable only to the extent that they draw the children closer to God and help them become more open and receptive to the liturgical life of the church, particularly the Mass.

If you plan to introduce any of these devotions or practices into your home or classroom, prepare the children beforehand. Help them to see the beauty in what you have to offer, and try to win their hearts to wanting to put these practices into their lives.

Many of the prayers and practices suggested throughout these pages have been handed down to us by our teachers and parents. They are not ours; they have merely been entrusted to us. We carry them, like the Olympic torch, only to pass them on.

The Rosary

More things are wrought by prayer
Than this world dreams of.
                    —Tennyson

For over 400 years the rosary as we know it
has been a major Catholic devotion. No other
prayer so comprehensively covers the entire
liturgical year and summarizes in its mysteries
the life of Christ and his Blessed Mother. In
spite of this, the devotion has been on the
decline since Vatican II. "It's the monotony of
the thing," people say. "Hail Mary . . . Hail
Mary . . . Hail Mary. . . ."

At the same time some who have laid aside
the rosary because of its "sameness" have taken
to Eastern devotions that have as their basic
technique the repetition of a word or phrase. I
once took part in such an Eastern prayer service.
Some 40 of us sat in a large, dimly-lighted
room—20 to one side, 20 to the other. Beginning
with one side, we recited a low, prolonged

"O-ohm-m," letting our voices rise and fall with the sound. When it died away, the other group took over. Then back again to us until a continuous wave of sound rolled from one side of the room to the other. After a while the swelling and fading of the hum became hypnotic, blending with the rhythm of our breathing and heartbeat. The purpose of the exercise was to keep the senses occupied so that the mind and heart could be centered on God.

The Hail Marys of the rosary serve the same purpose. We make no effort to concentrate on the words. Rather we allow them to form an ebb and flow of sound that keeps our tongues and ears occupied. Along with this we finger the beads to give our restless hands an outlet for their energy, and we involve the imagination with the mysteries. With our senses thus kept busy, the mind and heart are freed to be aware of God, of Jesus.

But, if praying the rosary has become too routine, what we need do is revitalize the devotion. We need to scrape from it—or from our own souls—the barnacles of boredom and pass on the restored and beautiful devotion to our children.

It is not enough to tell the children about the rosary. We have to prepare them to accept it. We have to speak with them about it, make it meaningful to them, tell them how they are to picture to themselves the various mysteries, how they are to think of Jesus and Mary and walk in spirit with them. Then we need to pray the rosary with them or at least show them how it is to be prayed and encourage them to practice it until it becomes a familiar and loved part of their prayer lives. Most of all we need to offer the children the example of our own devotion to the rosary.

What a triumph of faith, even though small, if someone, somewhere, would again start the custom of the family rosary. Not a worldwide crusade like Father Peyton started; that was his work. But a family here and there beginning again in a quiet, faithful way to pray the rosary together, would restore both family togetherness and devotion to the rosary.

Our changing social structures with their effect on domestic activities make this an almost impossible ideal. Where the children of the family are very young, it would be less of a problem. These small Catholics may not comprehend all that is going on when we gather them together and put them on their knees with a string of colored-glass beads in their hands; and their versions of the prayer may at times be less than orthodox. What matters is that they see us on our knees and know that we are talking with God. It's our example that counts. Those of us who can look back to the cold winter evenings when we knelt with the family about the kitchen range or around the big bed in our parents' bedroom during the warm summertime and prayed the rosary together, know that we have not only a treasure of happy memories but a source of lasting inspiration.

One last comment before leaving the theme. When we say the five decades of the rosary, even though we are not fastening on the words, we are asking the Blessed Mother 53 times to pray for us "at the hour of our death." While it is not wise to talk numbers when speaking of prayers, even children know the value of asking for something over and over again. They are constantly doing this with their parents—and getting results.

This matter of death and of our asking our Lady to pray for us when we die is a timely topic today when even children are coming to fear the possibility of dying in a nuclear war or by some other violent form. In the face of such fears, how consoling it is to believe and hope that, when that last hour comes for us, our Blessed Mother will remember that we have asked her hundreds of times to take care of us. Is it likely, after all those requests, that she will leave us alone when we need her most?

How to Pray the Rosary

By following the numbers
on the picture and the
corresponding numbers
of the explanation, you
can learn to pray the
rosary.

1. Begin by making the
   Sign of the Cross and
   praying the "Apostles'
   Creed."
2. Pray the "Our Father."
3. On each of these three
   beads pray a "Hail Mary."
4. Pray the "Glory be to
   the Father."
5. Think of the first Mystery*
   on which you wish to
   meditate and pray
   the "Our Father."

---

* We divide the whole of Christ's life into the five Joyful
Mysteries, the five Sorrowful Mysteries, and the five Glorious
Mysteries.

6. Pray 10 "Hail Marys" on these beads, but let your mind dwell on the Mystery rather than on the individual words of the prayer.

7. Pray the "Glory be to the Father."

Now continue praying according to numbers 5, 6 and 7, recalling the second, third, fourth and fifth Mystery at the second, third, fourth and fifth "Our Father."

The Joyful Mysteries
1. The Annunciation (The angel comes to Mary to tell her she is to be the mother of Jesus.)
2. The Visitation (Mary visits her cousin Elizabeth who is pregnant with John the Baptist.)
3. The Birth of Christ in Bethlehem
4. The Presentation of the Child Jesus in the Temple
5. The Finding of the Child Jesus in the Temple (Mary and Joseph find Jesus who was lost for three days.)

The Sorrowful Mysteries
1. The Agony in the Garden
2. The Scourging at the Pillar
3. The Crowning With Thorns
4. Jesus Carrying His Cross
5. The Crucifixion and Death of Our Lord

The Glorious Mysteries
1. The Resurrection of Our Lord From the Dead
2. The Ascension of Christ Into Heaven
3. The Descent of the Holy Spirit Upon the Apostles
4. The Assumption of the Blessed Virgin Mary Into Heaven
5. The Crowning of the Blessed Mother as Queen of Heaven

You may meditate on any of these Mysteries as you pray the rosary, but generally the Joyful Mysteries are used on Monday and Thursday; the Sorrowful Mysteries on Tuesday and Friday; the Glorious Mysteries on Wednesday and Saturday. The Glorious Mysteries are also used on all Sundays except the Sundays during Lent (Sorrowful) and the Sundays during Advent (Joyful).

The Prayers of the Rosary
Note: If you are praying the rosary with others, they may answer the part in italics. You will want to announce each Mystery aloud.

The Sign of the Cross
In the name of the Father, and of the Son, and of the Holy Spirit. *Amen.*

The Apostles' Creed

I believe in God, the Father almighty,
creator of heaven and earth.
I believe in Jesus Christ, his only Son, our
Lord.
He was conceived by the Holy Spirit,
born of the Virgin Mary,
suffered under Pontius Pilate,
was crucified, died, and was buried.
He descended into hell.
On the third day he arose again from the
dead.
He ascended into heaven,
and is seated at the right hand of the Father.
He will come again to judge the living and
the dead.
I believe in the Holy Spirit,
the holy catholic church,
the communion of saints,
the forgiveness of sins,
the resurrection of the body,
and life everlasting. Amen.

The Our Father

Our Father, who art in heaven,
hallowed be thy name;
thy kingdom come;
thy will be done on earth as it is in heaven.
Give us this day our daily bread;
and forgive us our trespasses

as we forgive those who trespass against us;
and lead us not into temptation,
but deliver us from evil. Amen.

The Hail Mary

Hail Mary, full of grace, the Lord is with you: blessed are you among women, and blessed is the fruit of your womb, Jesus.

Holy Mary, Mother of God, pray for us sinners, now and at the hour of our death. Amen.

The Glory Be

Glory be to the Father, and to the Son, and to the Holy Spirit.

As it was in the beginning, is now, and will be forever. Amen.

The Way of the Cross

*We adore you, O Christ, and we bless you;
because by your holy cross you have redeemed
the world.*

The church has always cherished devotion
to the passion of Christ. From the earliest days
of Christianity devout men and women have
sought out the path that Jesus followed to
Calvary and thoughtfully lingered and prayed at
the places made special because he walked there
carrying his cross.

Most of us will never get to Jerusalem to
retrace Jesus' footsteps to Calvary, but we can
stay close to him in his journey to Golgotha by
lovingly thinking of him as we make the Way of
the Cross in our churches. And what a priceless
gift we give to our children if we pass on to
them this same devotion.

The time of Lent lends itself to our intro-
ducing the children to the practice of making

the Way of the Cross or the stations. The pity of it is that often, after we have taught them how to pray the stations, they may not be able to carry on with the devotion because our churches are locked soon after the morning Mass; or, if they are not locked, it is not safe for the child to enter the empty church alone.

However, sometimes during the Lenten season, special church services include the stations. If the children cannot attend these services, it may be possible to take them to the church and make the Way of the Cross with them.

Again what is important is to prepare the children, to acquaint them with the devotion before they do the actual praying. Some of them may never have noticed the pictures along the walls of the church. We may have to call attention to them. A nun friend of mine, a primary teacher, was making the Way of the Cross one Saturday after Mass when one of her six-year-old pupils who lived nearby wandered into the church. He saw her and walked over to where she was moving from station to station. After a few moments he touched her arm. "They *are* nice windows, aren't they?" He hadn't seen the stations at all. He thought Sister was enjoying the sun lighting up the pictures in the stained glass windows.

The simplest way to prepare the children to pray the Way of the Cross is to talk with them about the stations. Take one station at a time and dwell on it. Tell them what is happening in the station. What we want to do is arouse in the child a spirit of caring about the sufferings of another and an attitude of humble gratitude that Jesus should have done this for us. If our words are to carry conviction, we ourselves need to think long and lovingly on the passion of Christ. Our own hearts must be warm with compassion if we hope to arouse this sentiment in the heart of the child. God grant us all such devotion.

The fourteen stations are:

1. Jesus is condemned to death
2. Jesus bears his cross
3. Jesus falls the first time beneath the cross
4. Jesus meets his afflicted mother
5. Simon of Cyrene helps Jesus to carry his cross
6. Veronica wipes the face of Jesus
7. Jesus falls the second time
8. Jesus comforts the pious women of Jerusalem
9. Jesus falls the third time
10. Jesus is stripped of his garments
11. Jesus is nailed to the cross

12. Jesus dies on the cross
13. Jesus is taken down from the cross and laid
     in the arms of his mother
14. Jesus is laid in the tomb

The Angelus

And the Word was made flesh.

The origin of the Angelus is obscure, but already in the middle of the 13th century the Franciscans—whose gentle founder gave us the first Christmas crib—had already begun the practice of daily reciting a Hail Mary to honor the Incarnation.

The prayer as we know it today goes back to the 16th century, to the time of Teresa of Avila, Cervantes, Michelangelo, Martin de Porres, Charles Borromeo. One can almost see them now—the mystic, the writer, the artist, the humble oblate, the prince of the church—all bowing their heads in prayer at dawn, at noon and at dusk as the Angelus bells rang out from the steeples of Christendom.

And the bells did ring for centuries— cathedral bells, convent bells, bells from city steeples, bells from village belfries and from chapels in hamlets hidden in the hills. It is only today that the bells are being muted, one by one. And with the silencing of the bells, the Angelus prayer is being forgotten, too.

It will be lost unless we pass it on to our children, unless we teach them to love and pray this beautiful prayer. But, here again, before we give them the prayer, we need to prepare them for it. We need to speak of the incomparable mystery that God should have become one of us. We have to get the children to dwell on the story of the Annunciation and the birth of Christ as we tell it to them from the gospel pages.

But the bare facts alone won't do it. We ourselves need to have spent time alone with the gospel story, to have set on fire our own hearts before we are ready to speak in believable words to the children.

And, when we speak to them, let us surround the story with all the beauty we can find. This shouldn't be too difficult. Beauty lends itself to the things of God. Think of the musicians, poets and artists who have dwelt on the theme of the Incarnation and tried to capture its beauty in their works. Make use of the fruits of their efforts. If possible, get a print of Millet's picture, "The Angelus." Show it to the

children. Point out to them the reverence of the
two peasants as they stop their work in the field
and stand in prayerful silence when they hear
the bells from the distant village church ringing
the evening Angelus.

Older children can, perhaps, be brought to
a greater appreciation of the devotion if they
listen to Schubert's or Gounod's "Ave Maria." If
they need something on a simpler level, there is
Carey Landry's "Hail Mary: Gentle Woman."
Fasten on anything of beauty that will inspire
them with a tender reverence and love for this
greatest of Christian truths. The human heart
hungers for the beautiful, the noble, for something above and beyond its reach.

We can't be satisfied with a one-time telling
of the Incarnation story. We need to come back
to it again and again, dwelling lovingly upon it.
Only then, when the children are ready, is the
time right to begin teaching them the prayer and
helping them make it a part of their lives. If we
are in a classroom situation, the Angelus can be
said with the children before the noon dismissal
for lunch.

The important thing in training the child to
a life of prayer is to act, to *do something*. It isn't
enough to sit by and expect the good to happen.
We must make it happen, fight for it, crusade
for it.

The Angelus

The angel of the Lord declared unto Mary,
And she conceived of the Holy Spirit.

Hail Mary. . . .

Behold the handmaid of the Lord.
Be it done unto me according your word.

Hail Mary. . . .

And the Word was made flesh;
And dwelt among us.

Hail Mary. . . .

Pray for us, O Holy Mother of God.
That we may be made worthy of the promises of Christ.

Let us pray:

Pour forth, we beseech you, O Lord, your grace into our hearts that we to whom the incarnation of Christ your Son was made known by the message of an angel may, by his passion and cross, be brought to the glory of his resurrection. Through the same Christ our Lord. *Amen.*

The Morning Offering

*O Jesus, through the Immaculate Heart of Mary,
I offer you my prayers, works, joys, sufferings of
this day in union with the Holy Sacrifice of the
Mass throughout the world. I offer them for all
the intentions of your Sacred Heart: the salvation
of souls, reparation for sin, the reunion of all
Christians. I offer them for the intentions of our
Bishops and of all Apostles of Prayer and in
particular for those recommended by the Holy
Father this month.*

Even if we ourselves have kept to the
practice of praying the Morning Offering, or
Daily Offering, we may want to rethink it before
we try to bring it to the children.

*"O Jesus, through the Immaculate Heart of
Mary"*—no matter what we offer to Christ, we
can be sure it will be pleasing in his sight if it is
through the hands of his mother.

". . . *I offer you my prayers*"—my acts of faith, hope, love, contrition, petition, the prayer of anguish that sorrow wrings from my heart, my prayers when temptation begins to blind my vision, the unspoken prayers that lie too deep in my heart to rise to my lips.

". . . *works*"—the never-ending round of household duties, the dishwashing, bedmaking, cooking, cleaning, getting the children off to school, feeding the dog, the work at the office, the constant answering of phones, the pressure of decision-making, the bookwork, the manual work at the shop or factory, the drudgery of its monotony, the work at the school, the tension of meeting deadlines, the long hours of study, or the endless correcting of assignments. All these I offer.

". . . *joys*"—each day brings with it a share of joy if nothing more than the joy of being alive. This, too, I offer.

". . . *sufferings of this day*"—my headaches, the raw sunburn I picked up at the beach, a head cold. But even more than these physical pains, the financial worries, concern about my job. And, over and above them all, the mental suffering and heartache of seeing a husband, a wife, a child suffer with no way of alleviating the hurt; the agony of experiencing a growing coldness between me and someone I love when

I don't know why it is happening. O Jesus, I offer these to you.

"*. . . in union with the Holy Sacrifice of the Mass throughout the world*"—I intervene in each Mass that is being said everywhere on this planet. Alongside the bread and wine on the thousands of altars across Christendom—in the ancient cathedrals of Europe, in the straw-roofed chapels in Africa, in the snowbound churches of the far north, on all these altars I place "my prayers, works, joys, sufferings."

"*. . . for all the intentions of your Sacred Heart*"—and we make bold to enumerate three:

> "*the salvation of souls*"—surely this intention must be close to the heart of Christ since he gave his life for that very purpose. And I, needing this salvation myself, move in with my prayers to say that I, too, wish to help save souls. I want to join in the missionary activity of the church. I want to bring people to God.

> "*reparation for sin*"—my own sin; the sins of my family, my neighbors, our parish, the town I live in; the sins of the men and women who people our prisons, who roam our streets and rape and murder and push drugs; the sins of the state, the nation, the world; sins of hatred, injustice, violence, abortion, fraud, perjury.

"the reunion of all Christians"—for many of
us the idea of ecumenism seemed to have
come into existence with Vatican II. But,
long before Pope John XXIII called the
Council, this intention was in the Morning
Offering.

". . . for the intentions of our bishops"—our
spiritual leaders shoulder the responsibilities
and burdens of church government in Christ's
name. This is particularly true of our chief
bishop, the pope. We want to back him and all
these shepherds of Christ with our prayers; we
want to let them know that we are with them,
supporting them. For all their intentions we
offer our prayers, works, joys, sufferings.

". . . and for all Apostles of Prayer"—I am
praying for you, and you for me, and both of us
for everyone else, millions of us praying for one
another, all saying the same prayer.

*". . . and in particular for those (intentions)
recommended by the Holy Father this month"*—big
broad intentions, encompassing the needs of the
world: the starving in Africa, the lepers, those
who are seeking employment, countries suffering from war. And the more spiritual needs:
that all of us may learn to sanctify our leisure
time; for Latin American Christians, that their
lives may be truly influenced by their baptismal
commitment; that married couples may use the

grace of the sacrament to remain faithful to each other.

I offer my prayers, works, joys, sufferings for all these intentions, for all these people, hoping that what I have to offer can change something for the better, bring about a richer quality of life for someone, further Christ's kingdom on earth.

But there's something almost audacious in all this. Who do I think I am—one insignificant individual out of the billions on this earth—to dare presume that anything I do, *anything*, could make a difference in the temporal or spiritual *status quo* of the world.

Of myself, what I do *wouldn't* make a difference. But the grace of God present in me brings the Holy Trinity into my soul. What I do then is not of me alone. It is not I who pray but God who prays within me. "The Spirit himself expresses our plea" (Rom 8:26). Nor do I work alone. "Whoever believes in me will perform the same works as I do" (Jn 14:12). Neither is my joy from myself for Jesus said, "I have told you this so that my own joy may be in you" (Jn 15:11). Even my sufferings are not my own. Like Paul, "I am suffering now, and in my own body to do what I can to make up all that has still to be undergone by Christ" (Col 1:24).

God does all these good works in me, and

these I offer back to him. What a magnificent prayer this Morning Offering then becomes, and what a treasure we have to pass on to the children!

Celebrating the Feasts and Seasons of the Liturgical Year

Make the feasts and seasons of the liturgical year meaningful to the children. With novenas no longer popular, with the splendor of High Masses a thing of the past and with the silencing of the bells announcing a feast, the church's holydays are in danger of being passed over or perfunctorily celebrated.

Do what you can to make these days come alive for the children. Speak of the feasts in advance and prepare the children by talking through with them the mystery that is being celebrated. Help them in every way to participate in the experience commemorated by the feast.

Make the children particularly conscious of the seasons of Advent and Lent. Suggest practices they might do during these days. Support and encourage any efforts they undertake. And don't hesitate to suggest acts of self-denial even to the very young. Remember the days when we went without candy during Lent and gave up the movies? No big deal in one sense, but in another it fashioned our minds to the spirit of the season and gave us the idea that something special was taking place in the church year. Best of all, we were motivated to do it because those who directed our small lives reminded us of how Jesus had loved us and suffered for us.

Dedicating the Days of the Week and the Months of the Year

A long tradition in the church has favored the dedication of the days of the week and the months of the year to special devotions: Sunday, the Most Holy Trinity; Monday, the Holy Souls; Tuesday, the Guardian Angels; Wednesday, St. Joseph; Thursday, the Blessed Sacrament; Friday, the Passion of Christ; Saturday, the Blessed Virgin Mary. The more common dedication of the months is March to St. Joseph, May to our Lady, June to the Sacred Heart, July to the Precious Blood of Christ, October to the Holy Rosary, November to the Holy Souls. We can capitalize on these ideas.

Of course, not every child will respond to each practice that we suggest. But, with so much to offer, we may hope that something will draw the child to a closer intimacy with Jesus or to a deeper spirit of prayer.

I owe part of my devotion to our Lady to just such a religious practice. During the month of May one of the nuns who taught in our grade school pasted a picture of our Lady onto the front chalkboard along with a thought or suggested practice. Each morning when we came into the classroom we saw a new practice for the day, something practical and not too difficult to be done to honor our Lady. The teacher said little about it, but all day before us on the chalkboard was that silent reminder.

Fostering Devotion to the Guardian Angels

The doctrine of the Guardian Angels is not explicitly defined as of faith, but devotion to the angels is rooted deeply in Catholic tradition. And the church does celebrate a feastday in their honor on October 2.

Pictures and statues of angels with their "broad white wings" are among our familiar childhood memories, and the "Angel of God, my guardian dear. . . ." prayer has long been a part of our everyday Catholic lives. We were taught to believe—and did—that these great and loving spirits protected us from physical and spiritual harm.

It may be true that the very young make little distinction between the angels and the good fairies they hear about in tales of fantasy. What matter? The writers of fairy tales have had good models in the angels, and time will provide a distinction between the two.

43

While popular devotion to angels has declined in recent years, we might want to ask ourselves if, in a world where Satan ostensibly exerts so much power, we are willing to let this devotion die out and have our children grow up ignorant of the comforting knowledge of these celestial messengers.

Drawing Names of the Saints for the Week or Month

You might handle this suggestion in a variety of ways. The names of the saints might be written on small slips of paper, and the children could draw a name at random. The difficulty with this is that, if your group is large and you don't want duplicate names, you may come up with some saints about whom little is known. Such saints usually have little lasting effect on the children's lives.

It might be more practical to gather a number of attractive stories about certain saints that you feel would appeal to your group. After reading the stories, you could have each child choose one of the saints as a protector or patron for the week (month, year). A spiritual exchange set up with a saint in childhood may blossom into a warm and loving relationship that lasts a lifetime.

Responding Prayerfully to Happenings Around Us

In training the children in piety, try to keep them from centering their prayer life on themselves. Wherever you can, have them move out from their own needs to the needs of others. One of the simplest ways to encourage this is to habituate the children to giving an inner prayerful response to what is happening around them. You might begin by suggesting that each time they hear a fire siren or an ambulance or a police car they pray for the people involved. A siren almost always means that someone is in distress and that someone else is hurrying to help. We can't be the ones giving the help, but at the sound of the siren we can say in our hearts, "Jesus, help them," meaning to pray both for the ones in need and for those rushing to give aid.

The sound of an airplane passing overhead can also be the occasion of a prayer. That plane is filled with people who hope to reach their destination. We don't know those people, but they are somebody's father or mother or brother or sister, and we hope God will protect them. "O God, give them a happy landing." It takes so short a time to say it, and yet it strengthens our sense of unity with others.

You might also encourage the children to make daily news items the subject for their prayers. Allow the students to bring news clippings or pictures of people and places that are suffering from some disaster. Post these on the bulletin board, and make them the focus of the children's prayers for the day.

At times allow the children to offer their own intentions. ". . . for my daddy who had to go to the hospital"; ". . . for my dog that got run over"; ". . . that I find my lunch money that I lost."

The teacher should be alert to the needs of the shy pupil who would like to ask for prayers but is too bashful to say anything: "Today Margie would like us to pray for her big brother who is leaving for the army."

Raising the Heart to God on the Hour

This was once a practice in some of our Catholic schools. Each hour on the hour, the teacher and the class paused for a moment of silence—15 seconds—to recall the presence of God. If you have never tried this, you will find it difficult to believe what a profound effect an interval of absolute quiet can have when it is dropped into the talk and activity of a busy class (or a hectic evening at home). A small kitchen timer makes a good monitor for marking the hour. It does away with the need to watch the clock.

In the self-contained classroom this was a simple matter. Today, with departmental teaching, you may be moving from one class to another on the hour and will need to adapt the practice.

Granted this pausing for 15 seconds interrupts your class. You will learn to cherish it.

Something happens in those few seconds that calms and revitalizes both you and the class. But, again, introduce this to the children only after meaningful preparation—and prayer.

Grace Before and After Meals

Bless us, O Lord, and these your gifts
which we are about to receive from your
bounty, through Christ our Lord. Amen.

* * * * * *

We give you thanks, Almighty God,
for all your benefits, you who live
and reign forever and ever. Amen.

When the Christian family used to gather around the kitchen or dining room table to eat, the saying of grace was a common practice. Father or mother would lead the prayer, and members of the family were expected to be present and in their places when the prayer began. At the end of the meal—and you stayed until the end unless you had a credible excuse for leaving—prayers were again said together.

Today it is almost impossible for all members to be present for family meals. We know this from our own experience. And some of us who do attend meals together in the house often leave before the rest of the family get up from the table. Whether this is a habit we've grown into or whether our new life styles make it necessary, the practice has affected our saying of grace.

One thing is certain: we will not easily change modern family patterns of living. But we can change ourselves. If we have grown slack in saying grace before and after meals, perhaps we can reconsider the reasons why we left off or are cutting short such a beautiful practice and once more bring it into our prayer life, particularly if we hope to encourage our children in the habit of praying before and after meals.

And it will be through the children, especially the very young, that we can hope to bring back these daily expressions of faith. If the children are taught almost from infancy to pause as they hear us pray before and after meals and if little by little they are instructed in the reason why, we can hope that the habit of saying grace will be established in them.

Prayer is speaking with God. And, while even the babbling of an infant can be pleasing to him, there is something to be said in favor of having the parent ask the blessing at meals. The child should pray along; but, if father or mother leads the prayer, the moment becomes of more sacred importance in the eyes of the child. If, on the other hand, the child is asked to lead the prayers before he or she is able to understand what prayer is about, the effect may be "sweet" or "cute" for the adults present, but something will be lost for the child.

If you feel that it is spiritually educative for the child to lead the family in prayer, set an age or occasion at which the child grows into this privilege, an eighth birthday perhaps or on the Sunday after his or her First Communion.

Since it is important that the child feel confident to handle this position of leadership, it is good to stay with a "formula" prayer. And what more simple than the traditional prayers for before and after meals? Any eight-year-old will have learned from his father or mother without much coaching: "Bless us, O Lord, and these your gifts which we are about to receive from your bounty, through Christ our Lord. Amen" and "We give you thanks, Almighty God, for all your benefits, you who live and reign forever and ever. Amen."

Even if the child has learned these prayers from listening to their daily repetition, we will need to talk through the prayer with the child, explaining the meaning and instilling a fitting reverence. Learning "by heart" should always

mean that our hearts are in what we are learning.

Whatever prayers we choose, let us carry
on our Catholic tradition of grace before and
after meals and lead our children along the
same way.

Morning and Night Prayers

Jesus, when I first arise,
Unto thee I lift my eyes,
Sign a cross upon my brow,
And my head in worship bow.

* * * * * *

Now I lay me down to sleep,
I pray the Lord my soul to keep;
And should I die before I wake,
I pray the Lord my soul to take.

Years ago it was common practice for the ordinary Catholic to roll out of bed at the beginning of the day and slip to his or her knees for a word or two with God, asking his blessing and protection. At night, one knelt at one's bedside, thanked God for the day, and asked his forgiveness for the faults committed.

Today, when the alarm goes off in the morning, a great number of us turn over in bed, flick on the radio, and crawl out from the covers listening to the morning news. At night a remote control device allows us to watch television programs until the last minute before we drop off to sleep.

The bewildering thing about our change of attitude toward morning and evening prayers is that we don't really know how it came about. We're decent Christian people, and once we had good habits of prayer, or thought we did, but somewhere along the line there was a gradual fade-out and now getting up to the radio and retiring with the TV seem the normal thing.

But what about our children? Are we willing that they grow up dominated by the news media? If not, if we plan to have them oriented to God and the things of God, we will have to start leading them along the ways of God when they are young since habits, religious or otherwise, are a matter of early training. Begin when the child is still an infant. Fold the little one's small hands together while you pray simple prayers aloud to God in its behalf. When the child is old enough, direct his or her first faltering effort in talking to God.

In establishing the child in habits of morning and night prayers, choose a regular time and stay with it as much as possible. A feeling of security follows on a time schedule. The hour becomes special because you make it special. The child senses that something worthwhile is happening since you drop everything else you are doing and take out time to talk with God.

Have a definite place, too, where the prayer is said. Perhaps you have a small shrine in the home, a crucifix on the wall, a religious picture that is meaningful to the child. You may want to light a candle or votive light to burn during the time of prayer.

From the start have the child take a reverent posture. While it is true that one can pray in any position, it is likewise true that outward reverence instills a similar inward attitude. The folded hands, the closed or lowered eyes, the respectful tone of voice, are all aids to devotion.

Make the child's first solo prayers short and simple. Rhyming prayers make an easy beginning. They seem to be psychologically in tune with the mentality of the very young. The swinging rhythm of the verses satisfies a child's love for singsong; and the heavy rhyme fastens the words in the child's memory.

I recall one such prayer I learned as a child. I quote it here both because it was inclusive of so much—thanks to God, sorrow for sin, petition for blessings, trust in God's care—and because I feel it is still a worthy prayer for young Christians.

Jesus, tender shepherd, hear me,
Bless thy little child tonight,
Through the darkness be thou near me,
Keep me safe till morning light.

All the day thy hand hast led me,
And I thank thee for thy care;
Thou hast warmed and clothed and fed
     me,
Listen to my evening prayer.

Keep me now from every danger,
Let thine angel guard my bed.
Thou hadst nothing but a manger
Where to lay thine infant head.

Let my sins be all forgiven;
Bless the friends I love so well.
Take me when I die to heaven
Happy there with thee to dwell.

Now I close my eyes so weary,
Fold my arms upon my breast,
Praying thee, my God, to bless me
As I gently sink to rest.
                    Mary L. Duncan

Several years ago there was a publicized
argument against the "Now-I-lay-me-down-to-
sleep" prayer. The contenders felt that the "if-I-
die-before-I-wake" idea frightened the child. My
guess is that the child is not even attending to

the words. The rhyme, the rhythm, the general notion of speaking to God are carrying the prayer.

Suppose, however, that the child does take note of the words. The lovely wonder of both these devotional poems is that they speak of dying in the Christian context of resurrection and life with Christ in heaven. How better to speak of death to our children?

Whether we choose rhyming or other types of prayer is beside the point. Let us choose *something* and carry it through with our children. Here, as in so many things the words of Proverbs are true: "Instruct a child in the way he should go, and when he grows old he will not leave it" (Prv 22:6). At least we pray and hope that will be true.

Crucifixes, Statues and Holy Images

One picture is worth more than ten thousand words.
—Chinese proverb

The tendency today is away from statues and holy images even in our churches. One valid argument has been that many of our devotional representations have been poor art. On the other hand our churches were never meant to be art galleries, and sometimes even a cheap print can raise the mind and heart to God.

If we are to believe that we are what we think, it is likewise true that most of our thoughts are influenced by what we see. If I raise my eyes to a blank wall, I usually register a blank in my thoughts. If my glance takes in a picture of a horse race, my mind corresponds with thoughts similar to the stimulus. If, when I

look about, I see a picture of our Lady or a
statue of St. Francis or a crucifix, my thoughts
are colored by what I am looking at.

Visual images can have profound effects on
us. This is even more true in the case of children whose imaginations elaborate on what they
see. A picture of a bear on a calendar in my
grandmother's kitchen once triggered a night-
mare for me and got Grandma out of bed in the
middle of a wintry night to assure me that there
was no real bear in the kitchen.

Even the saints found help in objects of
devotion. St. Teresa of Avila was converted to a
life of prayer by seeing a statue of the suffering
Christ. The Little Flower tells us that the grace
of healing came to her through the medium of a
statue of our Lady. And a crucifix became a
means of grace to St. Francis of Assisi.

Years ago there were small statues in
Christian homes and pictures of Christ and his
Mother and the saints on the walls. These
objects helped to keep a Christian atmosphere
in the house. It's hard to carry on a family fight
or an angry quarrel in a room where a statue of
the Sacred Heart or a picture of the Blessed
Mother is smiling down on you.

In presenting sacred images to the child, go
about it as you did with teaching prayers. Sit
down with the child and talk about the picture.

If it is already hanging on the wall, remove it and bring it close for the child to touch. Try in every way to make the message of the picture meaningful.

If you have no picture and are looking for one, keep the child in mind. Choose some simple, realistic pictures of Christ, Mary, the saints, something that will inspire devotion.

Introduce the child to the crucifix gently. We are so accustomed to seeing this symbol of Christ's passion that ordinarily the sight of it arouses little emotion in us. But the child is seeing for the first time this man nailed to the cross. If the little one has been taught to love Jesus, you may be amazed by the tender pity these small followers of Christ manifest for the hurting Jesus.

In all this early training of the child, keep your own heart tuned to the things of God, and you can be sure of choosing what best helps your child draw close to him, too.

Religious Songs

What will a child learn sooner than a song?
—Pope

Hymns are a powerful means of reaching the hearts of children and instructing them for good. The music fixes the words in their memory, and the beauty of the sound gives the words a deeper impact.

With the very young, the words of the song, as the words in the rhyming prayers, count for little. As the children grow older, the lyrics are of more importance. Since this is true, talk the words through with the children before teaching them to sing the hymn. Make sure that they understand what they are saying. At the same time don't hesitate to teach them a song that may contain a few unfamiliar words. Your learners may be eight- or nine-year-olds now, but they will grow into these hymns as they get older.

One might argue, and with reason, that songs with a challenging vocabulary ought to be reserved for a time when the child is more mature. This would be ideal except that sometimes upper-grade children take on a sophistication and/or a self-consciousness that keeps them from benefitting from what they might willingly have made part of themselves in a lower grade.

Some of today's hymns are patterned for the very young. Songs like "Hi, God" may fill a six-year-old's need; but, in trying to adapt religious truths to the child's mentality, we don't want to draw Christ, the Mass, and all their religious experiences down to a level where second-graders feel they know what it's all about. We may be in danger of destroying in our young Catholic population a sense of the transcendent, a sense of mystery, that demands a growing into and upward.

Go about the teaching of hymns as you did the prayers. Repeat the songs often enough that they become the permanent possession of the child. Usually this will be the task of the teacher since children learn most of their hymns after starting school. But parents can help. And it's a privileged child who has heard many of these hymns from the lips of his or her parents long before learning them formally in the classroom.

Christian Ideals

Lives of great men all remind us,
We can make our lives sublime.
                                    —Longfellow

The trend today is toward a horizontal spirituality. People want to hold hands—literally—as a community in happy awareness of one another. Witness the gusty hail-fellow-well-met kiss of peace in some parishes. Some of this stems from a healthy desire and understanding of corporate worship. Part of it may be an outward manifestation of an unconscious instinct to seek solidarity in a world haunted by global unrest.

Whatever it is, too much of the horizontal without a balancing of the vertical element in our spiritual life has robbed us of a sense of the sacred. A time was when we "looked up" to certain persons, places and things as being special, set apart, reserved as holy, different in a good way. We now have effectively pulled down the sacred to within our narrow dimensions.

Feast days, Sunday clothes, religious ceremonies, titles of respect, distinctive garb for priests and nuns, the person of the pope, parents and teachers as authority figures, all have been scrapped or removed from their pedestals. As a result we have a grand confusion of roles where all are equal whether they should be or not.

The situation has our young people bewildered. Many of them are reaching out to other religions, cults, groups that offer something above and beyond the horizontal, something that appeals to their hearts, stimulates their imaginations, allows their spirits to soar. We need to offer them persuasive patterns of Christian living within our tradition, models that they can imitate.

One way to bring these models to our young people is through good books. We can make such books available in our homes and schools, books about the saints and other worthy men and women who gave witness to Christ through their heroic lives.

At the same time we can't force the issue. The most we can do is have the books at hand. And who knows how the grace of God may work? A book picked up in a moment of idle curiosity has been the turning point in the life of more than one person. When St. Ignatius was immobilized with a broken leg, he read through all the romances in the house and then, for lack of anything better, picked up a book on the lives of the saints. God used that book as a channel of grace, and from that moment Ignatius' feet were set on the road to holiness. St. Augustine was helped to a better manner of life through the reading of a book.

With the very young the approach is simpler. You can put the books into their hands and have them look at the pictures while you do the reading. Choose books that are filled with illustrations. And when you read, take the child onto your lap if possible. The story becomes more real, more the child's own, if he or she touches the book, turns the pages, sees the print (even though it is still unintelligible). But, over and above these advantages, the feel of your arms, the closeness of your face, your voice, your breath, and the comforting warmth of your body reinforce the good message that the book has to offer.

The stories you read to the little ones need not always be of a religious nature. The saints are not our only models. Many men and women whose names are not on the calendar of the blessed can be worthy patterns for our children. And, while it may seem a move from the sublime to the ridiculous, the reading of fairy tales to children is an effective means of teaching them habits of virtue and developing in them the ability to distinguish between right and wrong, goodness and badness, nobility of spirit and baseness.

Whatever method or material we choose, we want to provide our children with models that will set their hearts on fire and make them want to reach for the stars. If we don't, someone else will furnish quite different models, and we may lose our children.

Holy Water

Wash me until I am whiter than snow.
—Ps 51:7

Holy water is a sacramental. Each time we devoutly touch our finger to it or are sprinkled with it, we are cleansed of our lesser sins. Think of the pattern of an ordinary day: the hasty unkind word, that perpetual impatience that bedevils most of us, our sloppy attention at prayer. How grateful we should be that the church offers us so simple and easy a way of cleansing ourselves from sin!

But, in working with children, we may have difficulty in getting them to feel the need of being cleansed from sin. We have stressed the idea of love to the extent that in many quarters sin is no longer regarded as a reality. Murder, rape, embezzlement—yes. But even these are regarded as something against the law of the land rather than offenses against the law of God.

We don't want our children to become scrupulous or overly fearful of God. But a sound, healthly awe of him is as wholesome and life-giving as the respect for authority that a loving child has for a caring parent.

God is good, and his goodness makes him lay down rules for our temporal and eternal well-being. If we choose to disobey these rules, we sin. It's that simple. And we need to make an effort to get through to the children that we are sinners, all of us, and we need forgiveness.

Holy water is not essential to this need. God forgives us the moment we turn to him in a spirit of repentance. But holy water is an external reminder to turn to him and actually *make* that act of sorrow. It is an outward sign that makes visible for us the invisible grace, a support to the physical part of our nature that may need something to help it keep pace with the spirit.

Preparing the child for a meaningful use of blessed water, then, is not an easy task. It is even harder today when this practice has been, in great part, abandoned both in the home and in the school. Years ago it was a common custom in many Catholic schools to have a small holy water font hanging on the door frame at the entrance to each classroom. As the children entered or left the room, they blessed themselves with the holy water, making the sign of the cross. And some boy or girl was always vying for the enviable job of going about each morning before the groups went to church for Mass and filling the empty fonts. The job's attraction, of course, included the opportunity of looking into each classroom to see who was there and getting in a few monkeyshines along the way. At the same time the small chore did carry with it the implication that something of importance was being taken care of.

Catholic homes also had their holy water fonts or bottles, and one of the last things that everyone did before retiring for the night was to bless himself or herself with the holy water. Parents sprinkled the little ones as they lay in bed. Holy water was also used in blessing when someone went on a trip or, in some homes, when the children left the house for school. And should a thunderstorm come up, mother could be seen walking through the house sprinkling holy water.

One has only to read the prayer that the priest prays when blessing the water to understand the significance of all this:

"O God, grant that this creature of thine (water) may be endowed with divine grace to drive away devils and to cast out diseases, that whatever in the houses or possessions of the faithful may be sprinkled by this water may be freed from everything unclean and delivered from what is hurtful. . . . Let everything that threatens the safety or peace of the dwellers therein be banished by the sprinkling of this water."

We are surrounded by so many evils today: the misuse of drugs, the cheapening of sex, rebellion against authority, lack of reverence for life, loss of the sense of the transcendent—evils that reek of the devil's presence—that we need all the supernatural help we can get.

At the same time many Christians today are reluctant to hear about hell and demons. Keep a positive attitude, they tell us, think in terms of love and acceptance and reconciliation and you won't need to bother about the devil or hell. That would be an attractive suggestion if it were not that willy-nilly the devil is a member of the cast and refuses to accept a minor role.

As for hell, anyone who has ever struggled with temptation can attest that at times it takes the threat of damnation to restore one's moral sanity. No matter how one looks at it, we do ourselves a disservice and delay our coming into the full beauty of truth when we try to reckon without hell and the Prince of Darkness.

Moreover, the threat is here and now and the attack is open. Satan no longer poses as an angel of light; he is up front, brazenly functioning in cults under his own name. And those who should know warn us that this is not just a fad of the '80s. It is actual spiritual warfare. The pope himself, in a 1986 series of summer sermons, made strong statements on the church's teaching about the devil, the first papal pronouncement on this subject in nearly 15 years.

So let us use holy water according to the intention the church has in giving it to us: to purify our souls of sin, to keep us from harm and to shield us from the devil. Let us encourage our children to carry on this practice with reverence and gratitude as a glorious part of their Catholic heritage.

The Scapular of Our Lady of Mount Carmel

He has clothed me in the garments of salvation.
—Is 61:10

Before Vatican II and the modification of religious habits, the members of many communities of monks and nuns wore a scapular, a sleeveless outer garment falling from the shoulders, as part of their official garb. The scapular was originally meant to serve as an apron; but, with time and the spiritual orientation of the monastic mentality, the garment took on the symbolism of the cross and the yoke of Christ.

For centuries lay Catholics have also worn a diminutive form of the scapular as a token of devotion. This scapular consists of two small squares of woolen cloth joined by strings and worn about the neck.

Tradition has it that our Lady appeared to St. Simon Stock in 1251 and promised him that anyone who wears this Carmelite Scapular—or the "brown" scapular as it is sometimes called—would be saved from hell and taken to heaven by her on the first Saturday after death.

The church has never officially made a pronouncement on this promise, but she has approved the use of the scapular as an expression of belief in Mary's intercession and of "the efficacy of the sacramentals in the context of a truly Christian life." This should be enough to encourage our wearing the scapular and reaping the blessings and spiritual benefits the church has attached to this pious practice.

What we need to remember for ourselves and for the children to whom we present the devotion is that the emphasis is not on simply *wearing* the scapular. One is to wear it with faith and devotion. If our Lady truly made the promise to save from hell those who wear the scapular, it was understood to apply to those who wear it devoutly. One does not wear the scapular as some good luck charm.

We have people like St. Alphonsus Liguori saying this about the scapular: "Just as men take pride in having others wear their livery, so the most holy Mary is pleased when her servants wear her scapular as a mark that they have dedicated themselves to her service." And Blessed Claude de la Colombiere says: "I

wanted to know if Mary really and truly inter-
ested herself in me. And in the scapular she has
given me the most tangible assurance." So we
are in good company when we devoutly honor
the scapular.

There was a time when classes of children
were enrolled in the scapular shortly after
making their First Communion. It will be up to
parents and teachers to see that our children
may once more benefit from wearing the scapular of our Lady. It will not be an easy task if the
practice has completely died out in our sphere
of action. It will mean adapting the story to our
listeners, making it credible while keeping it
within the boundaries of the church's approval,
stressing Mary's power with God for us and her
desire to help us use the sacramentals as aids to
salvation. No matter how we approach this task,
it will take on the dimensions of a challenge.

Again, our own convictions will be the
most effective tool in getting the children to
accept and love this ancient but ever timely
Catholic manifestation of love toward our Lady.

Part Two:

The One Who Bends It

We need not be saints to lead our children to God, but we should be trying honestly to become men and women of prayer—not prayer that has us on our knees all day but prayer as a life style. Such a mode of prayer is seeded in our acceptance of the people around us, of the things that make up our everyday environment, of ourselves, and of God; it is helped in its growth and flowering by our ability to live in the present and to command our choices.

Acceptance of Others

If our relationship with others is to be authentic, it must be one of acceptance. We need to accept and reverence people as they are and allow them to be that way even while we hope—and sometimes fall to our knees and pray—that what is unworthy in them will not hinder their eventually realizing God's purpose in their regard.

At the same time we need to realize that no relationship with another is ever static. I meet you, and a relationship is set up; five minutes later that relationship has changed; an hour later it has changed even more. In a sense I am never able to categorize you once and for all because you are always in a state of transition. The change may or may not be significant, but it is there. If some frightened Christians had secretly watched Saul of Tarsus ride out of Jerusalem on his way to smoke out followers of the Way in

Damascus, their judgment of him may have had some validity. The same judgment made several days later would have been false.

Because all of us are constantly in a state of becoming, we need to keep mentally flexible toward each other, not in some abstract way but in the reality of our everyday interchange with the variety of people who make up our small world: the co-worker who never returns the tools to the right shelf, the roommate who always expects someone else to clean the lint screen in the apartment dryer, the chronic offender who perpetually leaves crumbs on the butter.

In proportion as we are able to handle this reality in persons about us and as we respond with acceptance—awaiting God's fulfillment in them as we await it in ourselves—we will be building a foundation that will allow prayer to become our life style.

Acceptance of Things

Our acceptance of persons and our reverence for them is one way of drawing God into our everyday activity and fostering a prayerful life style. Our reverent acceptance of things is a further way. If we can learn to look on things as gifts loaned to us, if we can find the wonder in their variety and uniqueness, God will overtake us at every turn. There will be no need for us to seek him; he will jump out at us. We read in the life of St. Paul of the Cross that his reverence for things made all creation cry out to him. At times, as he walked through the garden and saw the flowers, he would tap them with the end of his cane and say to them, "Hush! Hush!" because they kept shouting so loudly, "God! God!"

This acceptance of things includes not only the material things about us but also the joys and sorrows that come our way. It will help us, when pain or trouble come, to see ourselves as a wire screen, a bit of meshed metal. We can think of the sorrow as a dense smoke cloud billowing toward us. What we don't want to do is step aside or seek to avoid it. We need to hold our ground, not stoically but loosely, gently, with arms open as it were, to give the cloud free passage. We are Christians and the cross of Christ has a purpose in our lives. But even as we allow the pain to sift through us in its completeness, we need to tell ourselves, "It came . . . to pass." Not to stay, but to pass.

We ought to do the same with joys. Most of us tend to blunt the ecstatic edge of our joys by gathering them to our hearts and holding them fast. We spoil the very things meant to give us pleasure. How much better to draw the sweetness from each drop of happiness that comes our way while allowing it to pass when its time is up, remembering that "we have not here a lasting city." If we can do this, pain and joy will both leave behind a residue of strength and peace.

This reverent acceptance of things and recognition of their place in our lives will begin to make everything about us full of God, and our life style will become a constant prayer.

Acceptance of Self

In training ourselves to be aware both of others and of things and to accept them as they are, we need likewise learn to accept ourselves. This means, in the first place, learning to recognize that our value lies within ourselves and not with the work we do. It will mean a struggle to apply this to our daily lives since the drive to succeed is so ingrained in the American work ethic that, when we fall short of our goal, we tend to consider ourselves failures. We are so accustomed to identifying ourselves with our work that, when it fails, we let ourselves go down with the ship.

It takes a great deal of detachment to throw heart and soul into a project—presumably for God—and not be eager to see it come to a happy conclusion. And there is nothing wrong in feeling that way. But, if we have tried, if we have given our best to the effort, we are successful no matter how the action terminates. It is the moment-by-moment fidelity to the duty at hand that counts.

This accepting of ourselves as we are reaches to all areas in our lives. We need to accept that we have just so much mental acumen for this or that field of knowledge, that our potential for learning certain skills or disciplines may be circumscribed by conditions over which we have no control, that we are intellectually inferior to some of our peers. On the other hand we should also accept that in each of us lie vast areas waiting to be developed.

The physical part of us needs acceptance, too. We ought genuinely to like and enjoy the way we look: our height, weight, hair color, contours, our general difference from others. This is not the same as saying that we should not do what we can within reason to enhance our appearance. If we are overweight, for example, even good health would suggest that we do something about it. But at any given moment we should try to give an easy acceptance to our bodily appearance. Often a sense of humor makes up for the lack of certain physical qualities.

What we want to avoid is refusing to acknowledge our limitations and trying to appear perfect. If we keep telling ourselves that we have to be perfect, we will be tempted to believe that any failure to measure up was due to some oversight on our part and that the next time we will make a better showing. Soon we will feel the need of always being perfect and, in order to keep up appearances, may find ourselves piling up excuses for our lack of excellence.

It's asking too much of human nature to be always perfect. It is much better to accept the truth of our limitations. At once we are freed from the need to constantly be proving ourselves. We can fail, and our failure will not surprise us. Rather, it will open the way for us to admit that of ourselves we can do nothing, but in God is our strength.

Acceptance of God

It is not sufficient that we accept people, things, and ourselves in order for prayer to become our life style. We need also to accept God and his way with us. There must be some space in our day when we stand completely idle before God in total surrender to him. The time can be spent in meditative prayer where we rest quietly in the presence of God. Or we can pray vocally using either our own words or those we find in devotional books or in the scriptures. Whatever we choose, the time must be completely for him.

One of the priceless lessons we learn in these moments of intimacy with God is the value of waiting. Whether we want to or not, we must wait for ourselves to grow, for others to move forward, for plans to materialize, for projects to mature, for dreams to come true. It is in quiet communion with God that we learn all this.

Such waiting has nothing in common with passivity. Rather, it is trying to pace our actions to the rhythm of the divine drummer within. To do otherwise, to try to rush the Holy Spirit and insist on our own tempo, is to destroy our chances of developing a prayerful life style.

Living the Present Moment

Prayer as a life style will become simpler if we learn to do what we are doing when we are doing it. This full attention to the present will keep us from slurring our actions as if they were of no importance. Slurring makes for unrest and interior dissatisfaction and causes us to feel fragmented and out of sorts with everything.

Try for one half day to give the complete gift of yourself to each action you do. This is particularly important in dealing with others. We need to give ourselves to them completely. This full gift of self is the basis of that reverence about which we spoke. Have you ever tried to discuss a matter of consequence with someone who continued to write or arrange things on his or her desk while you spoke? Do you remember how demeaned you felt, degraded, unimportant? Even when we are dealing with things, we owe them our full attention. If we fail to give it, we will never learn reverence for creation.

To do what we are doing puts us in command of our lives and prevents some external agent from controlling us and robbing us of our human dignity. It should be up to us and not to some force outside ourselves to determine whether or not what we touch will be turned into gold. If we choose, every act we do can take on the value of a sacramental. The 17th-century poet George Herbert says it well:

> Who sweeps the floor with high intent
> Makes that the action fine.

Freedom of Choice

If we are to become prayerful people and bring our influence for good to bear on our children, we need to develop the ability to freely choose how we will act. On the face of it, this seems to be stressing the obvious. Aren't we making free choices all the time? We like to think so; but, if we grow angry when we miss the bus or lose patience when we can't locate a letter we misplaced or rant when we find the gas tank empty at a time when we are already behind schedule, we are not so free in our choices as we might think. True freedom implies the ability to pause in the wake of a stimulus and choose how we wish to meet it. In this pause, this momentary hesitation, we allow a space for God to direct our choice.

Possibly our freedom of choice is most frequently threatened by time—or the way we respond to it. Our entire culture is conditioned by the clock. After a while this tyranny of time begins to tell on us. We get caught up in a general rush where one activity pushes another and the second a third until there seems no way to handle everything that ought to be done. The peaceful rhythm of life is disrupted, and we begin to feel out of harmony with people, things, ourselves, God. Only as we come to terms with time will free choices become possible.

An even greater hazard to our freedom is linked with our need for approval. We all look for a "thumbs up" response from others, and generally speaking, we need it. At the same time we want to guard against allowing the opinion of others to determine our choices. This may mean at times that we are going to appear foolish in the eyes of others, that we will need to stand up to the crowd and not back down at their ridicule. It is a hard line to follow, but it is vastly liberating.

One Last Thought

For those of us who bend the twig and who are reaching out to make prayer our life style, the challenge must always be: Are we earnestly trying to improve our relationships with others, with things, with ourselves, with God? And are we working toward that inner freedom that pauses in the face of a decision and allows time for God to indicate the choice we are to make?

As for the twigs we cultivate for the Lord, the children we spoke about earlier, are they better Catholics because of us? Do their lives give witness to the Catholic training we have given them? To paraphrase an exhortation heard frequently from preachers and religious writers: Can we assure ourselves that if our children were arrested and accused of being Catholics there would be enough external evidence to convict them?

If the answer to all these questions is yes, what a future there is for the church!